My Cookbook of
Cakes

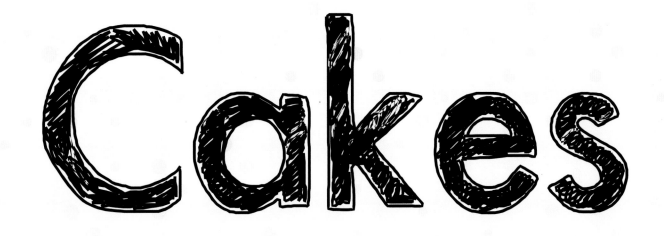

Laura and Jess Tilli

QEB Publishing

Difficulty rating

★ Easy peasy!

★ ★ Pretty simple

★ ★ ★ Getting tricky

★ ★ ★ ★ Chef's challenge

★ ★ ★ ★ ★ Super chef!

Always ask for an adult's help when you see these symbols:

 An oven or hob is needed, or a hot item is handled.

 An electrical appliance, such as an electric whisk is needed.

 A sharp object, such as a knife or grater is needed.

Editor: Lauren Taylor
Designer: Andrew Crowson
Photography: Catrin Arwell
Additional recipe testing by Judith Furtig

Copyright © QED Publishing 2012

Published in the United States by
QEB Publishing, Inc.
3 Wrigley, Suite A
Irvine, CA 92618

www.qed-publishing.co.uk

A CIP record for this book is available from the Library of Congress.

ISBN 978 1 60992 279 5

Printed in China

Serving sizes are approximations only.

All oven temperatures given are intended for fan assisted ovens. Standard conversions are given below:

Electric (fan) °C (°F)	Electric (no fan) °C (°F)	Gas mark
90 (190)	110 (230)	1/4
100 (200)	120 (250)	1/2
120 (250)	140 (285)	1
130 (265)	150 (300)	2
140 (285)	160 (320)	3
160 (320)	180 (350)	4
170 (325)	190 (375)	5
180 (350)	200 (400)	6
200 (400)	220 (425)	7
210 (410)	230 (450)	8
220 (245)	240 (465)	9

Contents

Techniques

Cream Whipping

Pour the cream into a big bowl. With a whisk, beat the cream as fast as you can until it becomes thick, but not too stiff. Be careful not to over-whip the cream, because it will curdle and end up looking like scrambled egg!

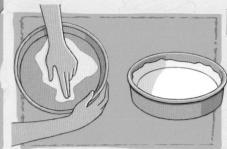

Pan Greasing and Lining

With your fingers, rub a small amount of butter all over the inside of your cake pan (this will make the paper stick to the pan). Draw around your pan onto wax paper then cut the circle out and place inside your greased pan.

Melting Chocolate

Put the chocolate pieces into a heatproof bowl. Put the bowl on top of a saucepan half full of boiling water. Turn the heat to a very low setting and stir the chocolate until it has melted. Turn the heat off and use oven mitts or a towel to take the bowl off the pan, as it will now be very hot.

Separating Eggs

Carefully crack your egg over a bowl and catch the yolk in your hand while letting the white run through your fingers. Put the yolk into a separate bowl.

Beating Eggs

Using a fork, beat the egg lightly until the yolk is well mixed into the white.

Whisking Whites

Tip your egg whites into a large clean bowl and use an electric whisk to turn them into big white fluffy clouds. You can use a hand whisk instead, but it will take a little longer, and you'll need more muscle power!

Zesting

The zest of a fruit is the very outer skin. Using a zester or a fine grater, rub the washed fruit up and down until flecks of zest appear. Avoid grating the white pith.

Folding

Very gently, move your metal spoon round the edge of your bowl then straight down the middle. Repeat until your ingredients are loosely combined. This is a technique used to combine ingredients without stirring all the air and texture out of them.

Apple Coring and Dicing

Stand your apple up and carefully cut each side off until you are left with a square core to throw away. Chop the four sides you cut off into even cube-shaped chunks.

Piping Frosting

Place your nozzle on or inside the end of your piping bag. Roll the bag down until it is half the size. Spoon in your frosting. Twist the bag closed and squeeze the frosting right to the bottom and into the nozzle. Carefully squeeze your piping bag from the top to make the pattern of frosting you want.

Spreading Frosting

Using a palette knife, spread the frosting over the top of your cake. Try to make it as even as possible. Next, gently glide your palette knife over the frosting in a zigzag motion from one side of the cake to the other. This will give the topping a finished look.

Rubbing

Rub the mixture together with your fingers until it looks like breadcrumbs. Don't rub for too long or your mixture will become too sticky and form clumps that do not crumble well.

Frosting for Cupcakes

Butter Frosting

Rating

Ingredients:
3 cups confectioners' sugar
¼ tsp salt
8 tbsp (1 stick) unsalted
    butter, softened
Colors, flavors or toppings

Equipment:
1 mixing bowl
1 sifter
1 wooden spoon
1 piping bag and nozzle
1 spoon

Preparation time: 10 minutes

Cooking time: none

Frosts: 12 cupcakes

1. Sift the confectioners' sugar into a bowl and add the salt and butter.

2. Mix until creamy. Add a couple of drops of natural food coloring if you want your frosting to be a particular color. Add any favoring you like. You can add a little water if your frosting seems too thick.

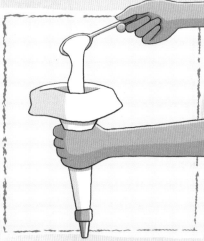

3. Place the nozzle onto the end of your piping bag and roll the bag down until it is half the size. Spoon in half of your butter frosting.

Tilli Tip
★ ★ ★
Make sure your cupcakes have completely cooled before frosting them.

4. Over your bowl, twist the open end of the bag closed, then squeeze the frosting right to the other end and into the nozzle.

5. Starting at the outside edge of the cupcake, carefully squeeze your piping bag and make a spiral pattern into the middle. Repeat with the rest of your frosting on each cupcake.

6. Add your decorations before the frosting dries.

Simple Frosting

Rating ★

Ingredients:
3 cups confectioners' sugar
3 tbsp water or juice
    of 1 lemon (this makes
    the frosting extra zingy!)

Equipment:
1 mixing bowl
1 wooden spoon
1 teaspoon

Preparation time: 5 minutes

Cooking time: none

Frosts: 12 cupcakes

1. Mix the confectioners' sugar with the water or lemon juice until you have a smooth paste. (You can adjust the thickness by adding a touch more liquid or sugar.)

2. Spoon onto the center of each cooled cake and let it run out to the edges.

Butter Frosting for Large Cakes

Rating ★

Ingredients:
6 cups confectioners' sugar
¼ tsp salt
8 oz. (2 sticks), plus 4 tbsp
   unsalted butter
Colors and flavors

Equipment:
1 sifter
1 mixing bowl
1 wooden spoon
1 palette knife
1 piping bag and nozzle

Preparation time: 10 minutes

Cooking time: none

Frosts: 1 large cake

1. Sift the confectioners' sugar into a large bowl and add the salt and butter. Miix your butter and frosting sugar together until creamy. Add any colors or flavoring ingredients you may be using.

2. Put your cake on a plate or cake stand. Place a big spoonful of the butter frosting on top of the sponge, then use a palette knife to spread it to the edges.

3. If you are making a layer cake, place your next layer on top of the frosted sponge.

4. Spread frosting on the top layer, making the coating as even as possible.

5. Next, use your palette knife to gently glide over the frosting in a zigzag motion from one side of the cake to the other. This will give the topping a finished look.

6. Place your nozzle onto the end of your piping bag and roll the bag down until it is half the size. Spoon in the rest of your butter frosting. Twist closed the open end of the bag, and squeeze the frosting right to the other end and into the nozzle.

7. Around the edge of your cake, carefully squeeze your piping bag in small spurts to make swirls. Apply more pressure when you start the swirl, then stop squeezing and pull it up to finish off, so that each swirl ends in a point.

8. Continue these swirls all around the edge until you meet your first swirl. Add any toppings you like.

You can change the frosting to any color you like!

Flavors, Textures and Toppings

You can add all sorts of ingredients to your frosting to make it even more yummy! Simply mix them in or add on top of the frosting before it sets.

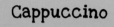

Cappuccino
Add a teaspoon of instant coffee dissolved in 2 tablespoons of warm water and sprinkle on a teaspoon of cocoa powder.

Peanut butter
Add a tablespoon of peanut butter.

Lemon
Add the zest and half the juice of one lemon.

Lumpy Bumpy
Add mini marshmallows.

Ribbons and Bows

You will need:

Assorted ribbons
Cocktail sticks
Cellophane
Colorful cupcake liners

- Using thin ribbon, tie tiny bows to the tops of cocktail sticks, then poke a stick into the top of each cupcake for a pretty party look.

- Wrap a length of thick ribbon around a circular cake and finish with a bow for a classic look.

Vanilla
Add a drop of vanilla extract to your butter frosting.

Chocolate Chip
Add 2 tablespoons of milk, white or dark chocolate chips.

Lime and Coconut
Add the zest and half the juice of one lime and 2 tablespoons of desiccated coconut.

Chocolate
Add a tablespoon of cocoa.

Strawberry
Add a tablespoon of strawberry jam.

● Place a single cupcake on a square of cellophane, and enclose the cake by gathering the cellophane corners together and tying with a ribbon—perfect for a special present.

● Use colorful cupcake liners to match your frosting and create a coordinated look.

Mini Candy Cupcakes

Rating ★

Ingredients:

8 tbsp (1 stick) unsalted butter
²/₃ cup granulated sugar
2 large eggs
2 tbsp Greek yogurt
1 ½ cups all-purpose flour
1 ½ tsp baking powder
¼ tsp salt

For the frosting:

1 cup confectioners' sugar
Juice of ½ a lemon
Variety of small candies and
    sprinkles, to decorate

Equipment:

2 mixing bowls
1 wooden spoon
1 mini muffin pan
24 mini muffin liners
1 teaspoon
1 wire rack
1 sifter

Preparation time: 10 minutes

Cooking time: 20 minutes

Makes: 24

1. Preheat your oven to 350°F (180°C). In a large mixing bowl, mix the butter and sugar together until creamy.

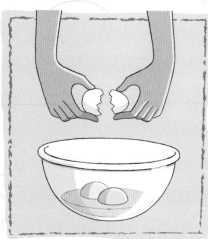

2. Add the eggs and yogurt to the butter mixture. Mix well. Add the flour, baking powder and salt and mix again.

3. Line your mini muffin pan with the mini muffin liners. Add a heaping teaspoon into each liner.

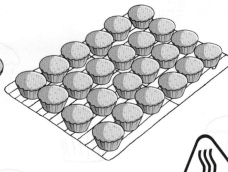

4. Bake for 20 minutes, until your cakes are golden brown. Leave the cakes in the pan for 5 minutes, then transfer to a wire rack to cool completely.

Jelly beans are chewy and colorful.

Tilli Tip
★ ★ ★
If there are only a few of you, why not halve the ingredients to make 12?

5. Sift the confectioners' sugar into a small mixing bowl. Mix the lemon juice into the sugar, a few drops at a time, until you have a thick shiny paste.

6. When all your cakes are cool, spoon a teaspoon of the frosting onto the center of each one and let it run out to the edges.

7. Before the frosting dries, decorate your mini cakes with the small candies and sprinkles.

Chocolate Peanut Butter Cupcakes

Rating ★ ★

Ingredients:

8 tbsp (1 stick) unsalted butter
2/3 cup granulated sugar
2 large eggs
2 tbsp Greek yogurt
2 tbsp crunchy
    peanut butter
1 1/2 cups all-purpose flour
1 1/2 tsp baking powder
1/4 tsp salt
1 tbsp cocoa powder

For the frosting:

1 cup confectioners' sugar
1/2 jar crunchy peanut butter
3 tbsp warm water

Equipment:

2 mixing bowls
1 wooden spoon
1 muffin pan
12 muffin liners
1 teaspoon
1 tablespoon
1 wire rack
1 sifter

Preparation time: 15 minutes

Cooking time: 25 minutes

Makes: 12

Try This!

★ ★ ★

If you're not a fan of peanut butter, try using chocolate spread for an extra-chocolatey cupcake!

You could try reduced fat peanut butter for a healthier option.

1. Preheat your oven to 350°F (180°C). In a large mixing bowl, mix the butter and sugar together until creamy.

2. Add the eggs, yogurt and peanut butter to the butter mixture. Mix well. Add the flour, baking powder, salt and cocoa and mix again.

3. Line your muffin pan with the muffin liners. Using a teaspoon and a tablespoon, place 2 tablespoons of mixture into each liner.

4. Bake for 20-25 minutes, until your cakes are firm to touch. Leave the cakes in the pan for 5 minutes, then transfer to a wire rack to cool completely.

5. To make the frosting, sift the confectioners' sugar into a small mixing bowl and add the peanut butter. Mix well. Stir the warm water into the mixture, a few drops at a time, until you have a thick paste.

6. When your cakes are cool, spoon the frosting onto the center of each one and let it run out to the edges.

Butterfly Cupcakes

Rating ★ ★ ★

Ingredients:

8 tbsp (1 stick) unsalted butter
⅔ cup granulated sugar
2 large eggs
2 tbsp Greek yogurt
1 ½ cups all-purpose flour
1 ½ tsp baking powder
¼ tsp salt
½ jar jam
Confectioners' sugar, to dust

For the frosting:

3 cups confectioners' sugar
8 tbsp (1 stick) unsalted butter
¼ tsp salt
1 tsp vanilla extract

Equipment:

2 mixing bowls   1 wire rack
1 wooden spoon   1 table knife
1 muffin pan   1 sifter
12 cupcake liners
2 teaspoons
1 tablespoon

Preparation time: 15 minutes

Cooking time: 30 minutes

Makes: 12

1. Preheat your oven to 350°F (180°C). In a large mixing bowl, mix the butter and sugar together until creamy.

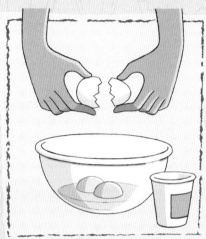

2. Add the eggs and yogurt to the butter mixture. Mix well. Add the flour, baking powder and salt and mix again.

3. Line your muffin pan with the cupcake liners. Using a teaspoon and a tablespoon, place 2 tablespoons of mixture into each liner.

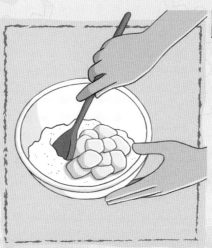

4. Bake for 25-30 minutes, until your cakes are golden brown. Leave the cakes in the pan for 5 minutes, then transfer to a wire rack to cool completely.

5. To make the frosting, sift the confectioners' sugar into a small bowl and mix in the butter, salt and vanilla extract until creamy.

6. When the cakes are cool, make the sponge wings. Carefully cut out a circle of sponge from the top of each cupcake and cut the circle in half using a table knife.

Tilli Tip
★ ★ ★

Wait until the cakes have completely cooled before trying to cut the sponge. Otherwise, you'll just make a mess!

7. Using two teaspoons, place a teaspoon of frosting into the hollow of each cake. Top with ½ a teaspoon of jam. Position your sponge wings on top and sprinkle on some confectioners' sugar using your sifter.

Use any flavor of jam you like!

Lemon Curd Cupcakes

Rating ★ ★

Ingredients:
8 tbsp (1 stick) unsalted butter,
2/3 cup granulated sugar
2 large eggs
2 tbsp Greek yogurt
1 ½ cups all-purpose flour
1 ½ tsp baking powder
¼ tsp salt
2 tbsp lemon curd
Lemon zest, to decorate

For the butter frosting:
3 cups confectioners' sugar
8 tbsp (1 stick) unsalted butter
2 tbsp lemon curd

Equipment:
2 mixing bowls
1 wooden spoon
1 muffin pan
12 muffin liners
1 tablespoon
2 teaspoons
1 wire rack
1 sifter
1 piping bag and nozzle
1 zester

Preparation time: 15 minutes

Cooking time: 25 minutes

Makes: 12

1. Preheat your oven to 350°F (180°C). In a large mixing bowl, mix the butter and sugar together until creamy.

2. Add the eggs and yogurt. Mix well. Add the flour, baking powder and salt and mix again.

Replacing the lemon zest with lime zest will add more color.

3. Line your muffin pan with the muffin liners. Using a teaspoon and a tablespoon, place 2 tablespoons of mixture into each liner.

4. Using a teaspoon, push a dollop of lemon curd into the center of each cake.

5. Bake for 25 minutes, until golden brown. Leave the cakes in the pan for 5 minutes, then transfer to a wire rack to cool completely.

6. To make the frosting, sift the confectioners' sugar into a small bowl and add the butter. Mix until creamy. Stir in the lemon curd and pipe onto your cool cakes. Grate over the lemon zest before the frosting dries.

Carrot and Orange Cupcakes

Rating ★★

Ingredients:

8 tbsp (1 stick) unsalted butter
2/3 cup granulated sugar
2 large eggs
2 tbsp Greek yogurt
Zest and juice of 1 orange
1 1/2 cups all-purpose flour
1 1/2 tsp baking powder
1/4 tsp salt
3 medium carrots, peeled and grated

For the frosting:

1 1/2 cups confectioners' sugar
3 oz. cream cheese
1 1/2 tbsp warm water
Ground cinnamon (optional)

Equipment:

2 mixing bowls
1 wooden spoon
1 juicer
1 zester
1 grater
1 muffin pan
12 cupcake liners
1 teaspoon
1 tablespoon
1 wire rack
1 sifter

Preparation time: 15 minutes

Cooking time: 25 minutes

Makes: 12

1. Preheat your oven to 350°F (180°C). In a large mixing bowl, mix the butter and sugar together until creamy.

2. Add the eggs, yogurt, orange juice and zest to the butter mixture. Mix well. Add the flour, baking powder, salt and just over half of the grated carrot. Mix again.

It may sound unusual, but orange and carrot are a great match!

Tilli Tip
★ ★ ★
When grating the carrots, make sure you leave a 1 inch (2 cm) length ungrated to avoid grating your fingers!

3. Line your muffin pan with the cupcake liners. Using a teaspoon and a tablespoon, place 2 tablespoons of mixture into each liner.

4. Bake for 20-25 minutes, until golden brown. Leave the cakes in the pan for 5 minutes, then transfer to a wire rack to cool completely.

5. To make the frosting, sift the confectioners' sugar into a small mixing bowl. Add the cream cheese and warm water and mix until creamy. Spoon the mixture onto your cooled cakes, and top with grated carrot and ground cinnamon (if using) before the frosting dries.

21

Rose-Petal Cupcakes

Rating ★★★

Ingredients:

8 tbsp (1 stick) unsalted butter,
⅔ cup granulated sugar
2 large eggs
2 tbsp Greek yogurt
1 ½ cups all-purpose flour
1 ½ tsp baking powder
¼ tsp salt
1 teaspoon rose water

For the frosting:

3 cups confectioners' sugar
8 tbsp (1 stick) unsalted butter
1 tbsp pink food coloring
1 tbsp rose water

For the rose petals:

12 rose petals, fresh and clean
1 egg white, lightly whisked
¼ cup granulated sugar

Equipment:

1 whisk
1 pastry brush
1 lined baking tray
2 mixing bowls
1 wooden spoon
1 muffin pan
12 cupcake liners
1 teaspoon
1 tablespoon
1 wire rack
1 sifter
1 piping bag and nozzle

Preparation time: 15 minutes

Cooking time: 25 minutes

Makes: 12

1. Preheat your oven to 350°F (180°C). Using your pastry brush, lightly brush each rose petal with egg white. Sprinkle the petals with caster sugar. Set aside on a lined baking pan for 2-3 hours.

2. In a large mixing bowl, mix the butter and sugar together until creamy. Add the eggs and yogurt and mix well.

3. Add the flour, baking powder, salt and the rose water and mix again.

4. Line your muffin pan with the muffin liners. Using a teaspoon and a tablespoon, place 2 tablespoons of mixture into each liner.

5. Bake for 20-25 minutes, until your cakes are golden brown. Leave the cakes in the pan for 5 minutes, then transfer to a wire rack to cool completely.

6. To make the frosting, sift the confectioners' sugar into a small mixing bowl. Add the butter and mix until creamy. Add the pink coloring and the rose water. Stir until the mixture is an even color.

7. Pipe the frosting onto the cakes. Once the petals are hard and dry, carefully place one on top of each cake before the frosting dries.

Tilli Tip
★ ★ ★

If you can't find any rose water, try using a couple of drops of vanilla extract for a different flavor!

Make sure your rose petals are very clean!

Chocolate Cupcakes

Rating ★ ★

Ingredients:

8 tbsp (1 stick) unsalted butter
⅔ cup granulated sugar
2 large eggs
2 tbsp Greek yogurt
1 ½ cups all-purpose flour
1 ½ tsp baking powder
¼ tsp salt
2 tbsp cocoa powder
¼ cup semisweet chocolate chips
Chocolate sprinkles and chocolate buttons, to decorate

For the frosting:

3 cups confectioners' sugar
8 tbsp (1 stick) unsalted butter
2 tbsp cocoa powder

Equipment:

2 mixing bowls
1 wooden spoon
1 muffin pan
12 cupcake liners
1 teaspoon
1 tablespoon
1 wire rack
1 sifter

Preparation time: 15 minutes

Cooking time: 25 minutes

Makes: 12

1. Preheat your oven to 350°F (180°C). In a large mixing bowl, mix the butter and sugar together until creamy.

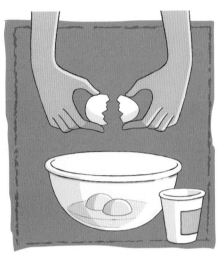

2. Add the eggs and yogurt to the butter mixture. Mix well. Add the flour, baking powder, salt and cocoa and mix again.

3. Fold in the chocolate chips.

4. Line your muffin pan with the cupcake liners. Using a teaspoon and a tablespoon, place 2 tablespoons of mixture into each liner.

Try This!
★ ★ ★

How about popping a square of white chocolate into the center of each cake before putting them in the oven?

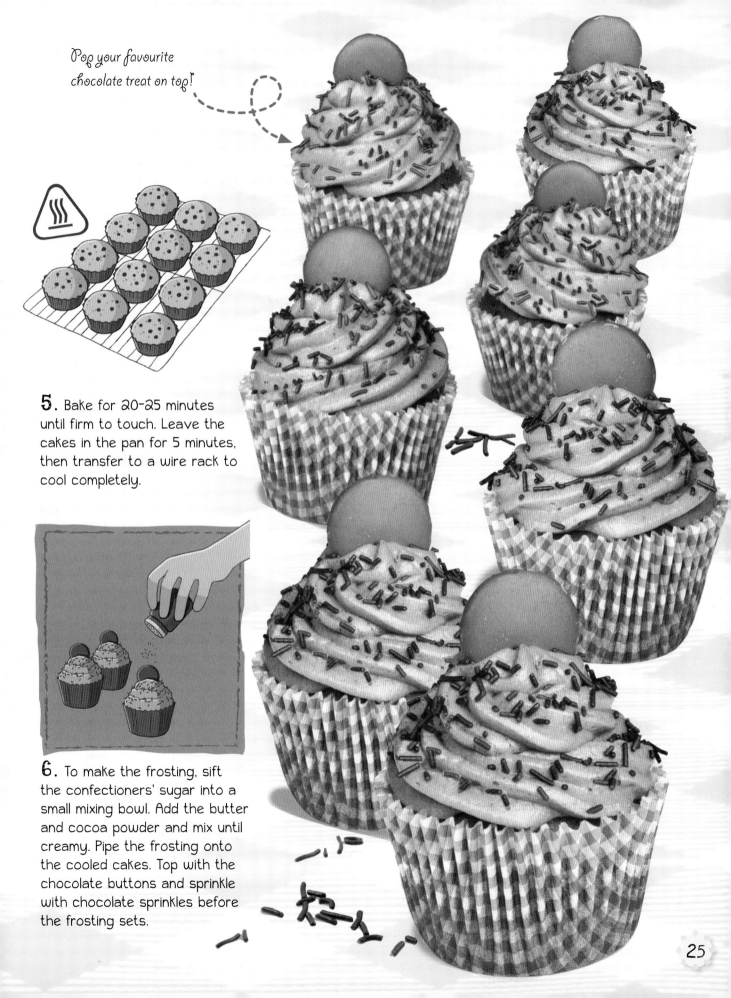

Pop your favourite chocolate treat on top!

5. Bake for 20-25 minutes until firm to touch. Leave the cakes in the pan for 5 minutes, then transfer to a wire rack to cool completely.

6. To make the frosting, sift the confectioners' sugar into a small mixing bowl. Add the butter and cocoa powder and mix until creamy. Pipe the frosting onto the cooled cakes. Top with the chocolate buttons and sprinkle with chocolate sprinkles before the frosting sets.

25

Christmas Cupcakes

Rating ★ ★

Ingredients:

8 tbsp (1 stick) unsalted butter
⅔ cup granulated sugar
2 large eggs
2 tbsp Greek yogurt
1 ½ cups all-purpose flour
1 ½ tsp baking powder
¼ tsp salt
2 tsp cinnamon
¼ cup dried fruit
Edible silver balls and
    confectioners' sugar,
    to decorate

For the frosting:

3 cups confectioners' sugar
8 tbsp (1 stick) unsalted butter
¼ tsp salt
2 drops of green food coloring

Equipment:

2 mixing bowls   1 sifter
1 wooden spoon   1 piping bag
1 muffin pan   and nozzle
12 cupcake liners
1 teaspoon
1 tablespoon
1 wire rack

Preparation time: 15 minutes

Cooking time: 25 minutes

Makes: 12

1. Preheat oven to 350°F (180°C). In a large mixing bowl, mix the butter and sugar together until creamy.

2. Add the eggs and yogurt to the butter mixture. Mix well. Add the flour, baking powder, salt and cinnamon and mix again.

3. Fold in the dried fruit.

4. Line your muffin pan with the cupcake liners. Using a teaspoon and a tablespoon, place 2 tablespoons of mixture into each liner.

Perfect for a Holiday party!

5. Bake for 20-25 minutes, until golden brown. Leave the cakes in the pan for 5 minutes, then transfer to a wire rack to cool completely.

6. To make the frosting, sift the confectioners' sugar into a small mixing bowl. Add the butter, salt and green coloring and mix until creamy. Using a piping bag, swirl the frosting onto each cake in a Christmas tree shape.

7. Sprinkle with the silver balls and use the sifter to dust with confectioners' sugar.

Tilli Tip
★ ★ ★

Wrap these little cakes individually in cellophane and tie with a festive ribbon – a great gift idea (see page 11)!

Easter Chick Nests

Rating ★★

Ingredients:
1 ½ cups water
1 cup milk chocolate chips
4 tbsp unsalted butter
7 cups cornflakes
2 tbsp golden syrup or dark
   corn syrup
36 small chocolate eggs and
   12 fluffy chicks, to decorate

Equipment:
1 saucepan
1 heatproof mixing bowl
1 wooden spoon
1 muffin pan
12 cupcake liners
1 tablespoon

Preparation time: 20 minutes

Cooking time: 5 minutes

Makes: 12

1. Pour the water into the saucepan. Carefully bring to a boil. Turn down the heat until the water is simmering.

2. Put the chocolate and butter in the heatproof mixing bowl and rest it on the pan, over the simmering water. Stir until melted.

3. Using oven mitts, take the bowl off the heat. Add the cornflakes and syrup. Mix well.

4. Line your muffin pan with the cupcake liners. Fill each with 2 tablespoons of the crunchy mixture. Make a dip in the middle of each nest with the back of the spoon.

5. Place three chocolate eggs into each hollow in the nests. Transfer to the refrigerator for about 2 hours until firm. Add a fluffy chick to each nest before serving.

A great alternative to Easter eggs!

Try This!
★ ★ ★
Why not try making one big nest? Use the same ingredients but fill one large round cake pan. Perfect for sharing!

Mother's Day Cake

Rating ★★★

Ingredients:
1 cup (2 sticks), plus 4 tbsp
   unsalted butter
1 ½ cups granulated sugar
4 large eggs
2 tsp vanilla extract
2 tbsp Greek yogurt
2 cups all-purpose flour
2 tsp baking powder
½ tsp salt
Clean, fresh flowers, to decorate

For the frosting:
1 lb. confectioners' sugar
8 oz. (2 sticks) unsalted butter
½ jar good-quality lemon curd

Equipment:
2 mixing bowls
1 wooden spoon
2 (8-inch) springform pans
1 wire rack
1 serving plate
1 sifter
1 palette knife
1 piping bag and nozzle

Preparation time: 25 minutes

Cooking time: 30 minutes

Serves: about 12

1. Preheat oven to 350°F (180°C). In a large mixing bowl, mix together butter and sugar until creamy.

2. Add eggs, vanilla extract and yogurt to the butter mixture. Mix well.

3. Add the flour, baking powder and salt. Mix until you have a smooth batter.

4. Divide the mixture between the two pans. Bake both for 25–30 minutes, until golden brown and springy to touch.

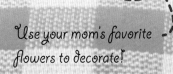

Use your mom's favorite flowers to decorate!

5. Leave the cakes in the pans for 5 minutes. Turn the cakes out onto a wire rack, peel off the paper and leave to cool completely.

6. For the frosting, sift the confectioners' sugar into a small bowl then mix in the butter until creamy. Using a palette knife, spread a layer of frosting over one of the cakes, then add a layer of lemon curd on top. Place the second cake on top and ice.

7. Pipe swirls of frosting around the edge of your cake. Finally, decorate with fresh flowers.

Tilli Tip
★ ★ ★
If your mom isn't keen on lemon curd, you could always swap it for a fruity jam or even just leave it out! It'll still be yummy!

Halloween Spider Cupcakes

Rating ★★★★★

Ingredients:

8 tbsp (1 stick) unsalted butter
2/3 cup granulated sugar
2 large eggs
2 tbsp Greek yogurt
1 ½ cups all-purpose flour
1 ½ tsp baking powder
¼ tsp salt
Orange sprinkles, to decorate
Small candies, for the eyes
24 red licorice laces, cut into
    quarters for the legs

For the frosting:

1 ¼ cups confectioners' sugar
8 tbsp (1 stick) unsalted butter
¼ tsp salt
2 drops of black food coloring

Equipment:

2 mixing bowls   1 sifter
1 teaspoon   1 piping bag
1 tablespoon   and nozzle
1 wooden spoon
1 muffin pan
12 muffin liners
1 wire rack

Preparation time: 25 minutes

Cooking time: 25 minutes

Makes: 12

1. Preheat oven to 350°F (180°C). In a large mixing bowl, mix together butter and sugar until creamy.

2. Add the eggs and yogurt to the butter mixture. Mix well. Add the flour, baking powder and salt and mix again.

3. Line your muffin pan with the cupcake liners. Using a teaspoon and a tablespoon, place 2 tablespoons of mixture into each liner.

These are almost too scary to eat!

Tilli Tip

★ ★ ★

Don't cut the spiders' legs too long, or you will have trouble sticking them to the frosting.

4. Bake for 20-25 minutes, until golden brown. Leave the cakes in the pans for 5 minutes, then transfer to a wire rack to cool completely.

5. To make the frosting, sift the confectioners' sugar into a small mixing bowl. Add the butter, salt and black food coloring and mix until creamy. Pipe a swirl of frosting onto each cake.

6. Scatter over the orange sprinkles, Add two candies to each cake to make the spiders' scary eyes!

7. Stick four red licorice lace quarters onto either side of each cake to make the legs.

Pumpkin and White Chocolate Bars

Rating  ★ ★

Ingredients:
¾ cup (1 ½ sticks) unsalted butter
1 ½ cups granulated sugar
3 large eggs
2 tbsp Greek yogurt
2 cups all-purpose flour
2 ¼ tsp baking powder
½ tsp salt
2 tsp cinnamon
1 lb. peeled fresh pumpkin or
　　sweet potato, grated
1 ¼ cups white chocolate chips
Zest and juice of 1 orange
1 cup white chocolate chips,
　　melted, for drizzling

Equipment:
1 mixing bowl
1 wooden spoon
1 grater
1 9 x 13-inch pan
1 tablespoon

Preparation time: 15 minutes

Cooking time: 45 minutes

Makes: about 12–16

1. Preheat oven to 350°F (180°C). In a mixing bowl, mix together the butter and sugar until creamy.

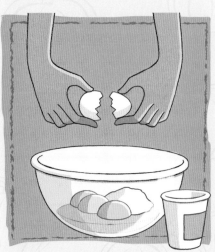

2. Add the eggs and yogurt to the butter mixture. Mix again.

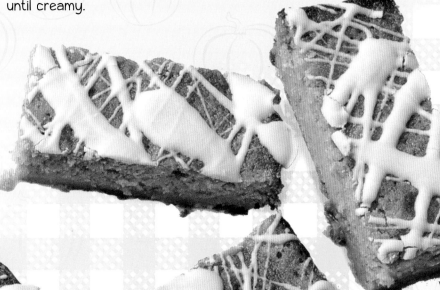

Milk or dark chocolate would do just as well for drizzling.

Tilli Tip

★ ★ ★

Make sure you ask an adult to help you peel and grate the pumpkin – they can be very tough!

3. Mix in flour, baking powder, salt and cinnamon. Add all the other ingredients, except the white chocolate for drizzling, and mix again.

4. Pour the mixture into a lined pan and spread it out evenly. Bake for 40-45 minutes, until golden brown.

5. Leave the cake to cool completely in the pan. Then, using a tablespoon, drizzle over the white chocolate. Let the chocolate set. Remove the cake from the pan, peel off the paper and cut into slices.

Easy-Peasy Birthday Cake

Rating ⭐ ⭐ ⭐

Ingredients:

1 cup (2 sticks) plus 4 tbsp
   unsalted butter
1 ½ cups granulated sugar
2 large eggs
2 tbsp Greek yogurt
2 cups all-purpose flour
1 tsp baking powder
¼ tsp salt
Cookies and candles, to decorate

For the frosting:

7 cups confectioners' sugar
14 tbsp unsalted butter
½ tsp salt
¼ cup milk or orange juice
2 tsp vanilla extract

Equipment:

2 mixing bowls   1 palette knife
1 wooden spoon   1 piping bag
1 wire rack   and nozzle
2 (8-inch)   1 sifter
   springform pans

Preparation time: 25 minutes

Cooking time: 20–25 minutes

Serves: about 8–10

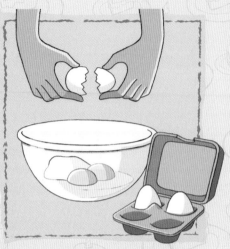

1. Preheat oven to 350°F (180°C). In a large mixing bowl, mix together the butter and sugar until creamy.

2. Add the eggs and yogurt to the butter mixture. Mix again. Add the flour, baking powder and salt and mix until you have a smooth batter.

3. Divide the mixture between the two pans. Bake for 20-25 minutes, until golden brown.

4. Leave the cakes in the pans for 5 minutes. Turn the cakes out onto a wire rack, peel off the paper and leave to cool completely.

Tilli Tip
★ ★ ★
Palette knives are much bigger and flatter than table knives, making them better for spreading frosting.

5. To make the frosting, sift the confectioners' sugar into a small mixing bowl. Then mix in the butter, salt, milk and vanilla extract until smooth. Spread about a third of the frosting on one of the cakes. Sandwich together with the other layer.

6. Using a palette knife, spread the rest of the frosting all over the cake. Make sure you reserve some for piping on top.

7. Pipe frosting swirls around the edge of your cake and decorate with cookies around the sides. Finally, add candles on top. Happy Birthday!

Use the birthday girl's or boy's favorite biscuits!

Striped Layer Cake

Rating ★★★★★

Ingredients:

2 cups (4 sticks) unsalted butter
2 ¼ cups granulated sugar
6 large eggs
2 tbsp Greek yogurt
3 cups all-purpose flour
2 tsp baking powder
1 tsp salt
Few drops of pink food coloring
Mini marshmallows and sprinkles,
    to decorate

For the frosting:

6 cups confectioners' sugar
8 oz. (2 sticks) plus 4 tbsp
    unsalted butter
¼ tsp salt
2 tsp vanilla extract
2 tsp pink food coloring

Equipment:

3 mixing bowls   1 tablespoon
1 wooden spoon   1 piping bag
1 electric whisk   and nozzle
2 round (8-inch)
    springform pans
2 small bowls
1 wire rack
1 serving plate
1 sifter
1 palette knife

Preparation time: 30 minutes

Cooking time: 40-50 minutes

Serves: 8–10

1. Preheat oven to 350°F (180°C). In a large mixing bowl, mix the butter and sugar together until creamy. Add the eggs and yogurt. Mix again.

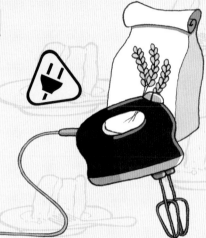

2. Add the flour, baking powder and salt and mix well. An electric whisk could help, if you have one.

3. Line up your cake pans and two small bowls. Divide your mixture equally between your pans and bowls.

4. Bake the batter in the pans for 20-25 minutes, until golden brown. Meanwhile, add 2 drops of pink food coloring to each bowl of batter. Stir well.

Change the frosting to any color you like!

5. When your first two cakes are cooked, leave them in their pans for 5 minutes. Turn them out onto a wire rack to cool completely. Clean, grease and line your pans again, and repeat with the pink cake mixture.

6. Sift the confectioners' sugar and mix it with the butter, salt and vanilla extract in a small mixing bowl. Transfer a few tablespoons of the frosting to a separate bowl and stir in the pink food coloring. Layer the cakes (white, pink, white, pink), with white frosting spread between each layer and on top.

7. Using a piping bag, pipe pink swirls of frosting around the edge of the cake. Dot marshmallows around the top and scatter with sprinkles.

Try This
★ ★ ★
Instead of marshmallows, you could use your favorite candies for the topping.

Zesty Glazed Orange Cake

Rating ★★

Ingredients:

¾ cup (1 ½ sticks) unsalted butter
¾ cup granulated sugar
2 large eggs
1 tbsp Greek yogurt
1 ½ cups all-purpose flour
2 ½ tsp baking powder
¼ tsp tsp salt
½ cup ground almonds
Juice and zest of 1 orange

For the glaze:

Juice of 1 orange
3 tbsp granulated sugar

Equipment:

1 mixing bowl   1 toothpick
1 wooden spoon   1 small pan
1 zester
1 juicer
9 x 5-inch loaf pan,
    greased and lined

Preparation time: 15 minutes

Cooking time: 35–40 minutes

Serves: 8–10

1. Preheat oven to 350°F (180°C). In a mixing bowl, mix together the butter and sugar until creamy.

2. Add the eggs and yogurt to the butter mixture. Mix well. Add the flour, salt, almonds and baking powder. Mix again. Stir in the orange juice and zest.

3. Pour the batter into the loaf pan and bake for 35–40 minutes, or until a skewer inserted into the cake comes out clean.

4. To make the glaze, carefully heat the orange juice and sugar in a small pan, until all the sugar has dissolved.

5. Using a toothpick, poke holes into the top of the cake and drizzle the orange glaze all over.

Tilli Tip
★ ★ ★

Heat the glaze gently, without boiling it, or it may burn

Lemon instead of orange will taste great too!

6. Leave the cake to cool in the pan before removing. Peel off the paper and cut into slices.

Chocolate Swiss Roll

Ingredients:

Splash of olive oil,
    for greasing
4 large eggs
½ cup granulated sugar
¾ cup all-purpose flour
2 tbsp cocoa powder
½ jar chocolate spread
1 packet mini marshmallows
Confectioners' sugar, to dust

Equipment:

jelly roll pan
parchment paper
1 mixing bowl
1 whisk
1 sifter
1 tablespoon
1 palette knife

Preparation time: 25 minutes

Cooking time: 15 minutes

Serves: 8–10

1. Preheat oven to 350°F (180°C). Grease the jelly roll pan with the olive oil, then line it.

2. In a mixing bowl, whisk together the eggs and sugar until light and fluffy.

3. Sift the flour and cocoa powder over the egg mixture. Carefully fold in.

Dust with more cocoa powder instead for extra chocolatey goodness!

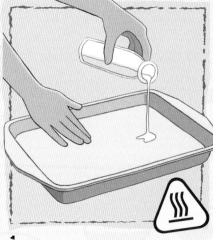

4. Pour the mixture into the pan. Bake for 15 minutes, until the cake is springy to touch.

5. Cut out a piece of parchment paper that is slightly bigger than the jelly roll pan. Lay it on a work surface and dust with confectioners' sugar. Gently tip the sponge onto the paper. Peel off the paper already on the sponge and leave it to cool.

6. Using a palette knife, cover the sponge with chocolate spread. Sprinkle with the mini marshmallows. Using the paper to help, carefully roll the cake into a long sausage shape. Finally, dust with confectioners' sugar and cut into yummy slices.

Try This!
★ ★ ★
Replace the chocolate spread and marshmallows with whipped cream and chopped strawberries.

Tangy Lemon Cake

Rating ★ ★

Ingredients:
1 cup (2 sticks) plus 4 tbsp
    unsalted butter
1 ½ cups granulated sugar
4 large eggs
2 tbsp Greek yogurt
Juice and zest of 1 lemon
2 cups all-purpose flour
2 tsp baking powder
½ tsp salt
Zest of ½ lemon, to decorate

For the frosting:
2 cups confectioners' sugar
4 tbsp unsalted butter
¼ tsp salt
Juice and zest of ½ lemon

Equipment:
2 mixing bowls   1 sifter
1 wooden spoon   1 serving plate
1 juicer   1 palette knife
1 zester
1 whisk
2 (8-inch) springform
    pans, greased and lined
1 wire rack

Preparation time: 25 minutes

Cooking time: 25 minutes

Serves: 8–10

1. Preheat oven to 350°F (180°C). Mix the butter and sugar together in a large mixing bowl until creamy.

2. Add the eggs, yogurt, lemon juice and zest to the butter mixture. Whisk together. Add the flour and whisk again until light and fluffy.

A zigzag effect on the frosting will give your cake a finished look.

3. Separate the mixture between the two pans Bake for 20–25 minutes, until golden brown.

Try This!

You could use limes instead of lemons—then your cake will be even more tangy!

4. Leave the cakes to cool in their pans for 5 minutes. Turn the cakes out onto a wire rack, peel the paper off and leave to cool completely.

5. To make the frosting, sift the confectioners' sugar into a small bowl, then add the butter, salt, lemon juice and zest and mix until creamy.

6. Using a palette knife, spread the frosting on top of one cake. Place the unfrosted cake on top of the other and spread more frosting on top. Sprinkle over with lemon zest.

Banana and Honey Cake

Rating ⭐⭐

Ingredients:
10 tbsp unsalted butter
⅔ cup granulated sugar
2 large eggs
1 tbsp honey
1 very ripe banana, mashed
⅔ cup all-purpose flour
1 ¼ tsp baking powder
¼ tsp salt
½ cup wheat bran
¼ cup roasted, shelled
    pumpkin seeds
1 tbsp confectioners' sugar,
    to dust

Equipment:
1 mixing bowl   1 toothpick
1 wooden spoon   1 sifter
1 potato masher
9-inch square baking pan,
    greased and lined

Preparation time: 15 minutes

Cooking time: 35–40 minutes

Serves: 12–16

1. Preheat oven to 350°F (180°C). Mix the butter and sugar together until creamy.

2. Add the eggs, honey and banana to the butter mixture. Mix again.

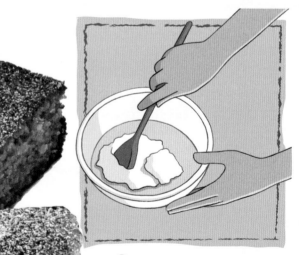

3. Mix in the flour, baking powder, salt and bran until the mixture is smooth.

Perfect for a summer picnic!

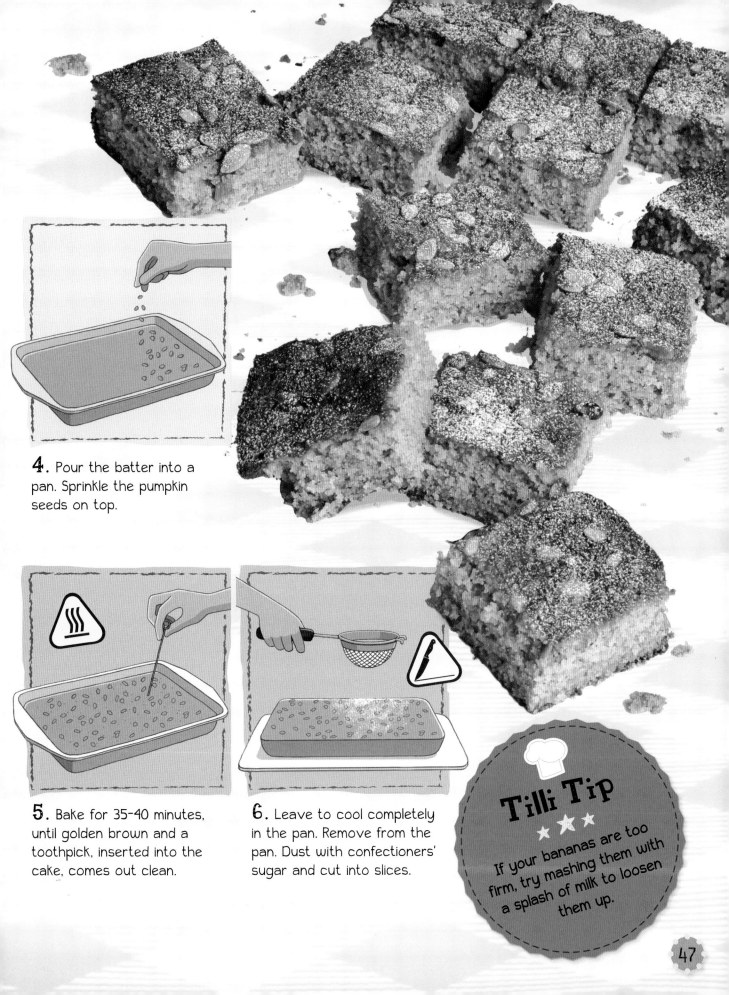

4. Pour the batter into a pan. Sprinkle the pumpkin seeds on top.

5. Bake for 35-40 minutes, until golden brown and a toothpick, inserted into the cake, comes out clean.

6. Leave to cool completely in the pan. Remove from the pan. Dust with confectioners' sugar and cut into slices.

Tilli Tip
★ ★ ★

If your bananas are too firm, try mashing them with a splash of milk to loosen them up.

Apricot No-Bake Cake

Rating ★ ★

Ingredients:

¾ cup of your favorite cookies
1 ¼ cups water
10 oz. milk chocolate
½ cup (1 stick) unsalted butter
4 tbsp dark corn syrup
⅔ cup chopped, dried apricots
1 large handful of pumpkin seeds

Equipment:

1 large sandwich or freezer bag
1 rolling pin
1 saucepan
1 heatproof mixing bowl
1 wooden spoon
1 9 x 13-inch baking pan,
  greased and well lined
1 spatula

Preparation time: 20 minutes

Cooking time: 5 minutes

Serves: 16–20

1. Seal your cookies in a large sandwich or freezer bag, making sure there is as little air inside as possible. Using a rolling pin, crush them into small pieces.

2. Pour water in the saucepan. Carefully bring to a boil. Turn down the heat and let the water simmer.

Tilli Tip
★ ★ ★
Butter cookies or ginger snaps work particularly well in this cake!

3. Break the chocolate into small pieces and put them into the mixing bowl with the butter and syrup. Carefully rest the bowl on top of the simmering pan of water. Stir until the chocolate has melted and the mixture is smooth. Turn off the heat and, using oven gloves, remove the bowl from the pan.

4. Add the crushed biscuits, apricots and pumpkin seeds to the mixture. Mix well.

5. Make sure the parchment paper in your pan goes up the sides, so it is easy to lift the cake out. Pour the mixture into the tray, using the spatula to spread it right into the corners.

6. Place in the refrigerator for 2–4 hours. Once firm, lift the cake out of the pan and cut into slices.

Eat with a napkin—these are deliciously gooey!

Banoffee Cake

Rating ★ ★ ★

Ingredients:

1 cup (2 sticks) plus 4 tbsp
   unsalted butter
1 ½ cups granulated sugar
4 large eggs
2 tbsp Greek yogurt
1 tsp vanilla extract
2 cups all-purpose flour
2 tsp baking powder
½ tsp salt
1 (14 oz.) can dulce de leche
2 bananas, sliced
1 cup heavy cream, whipped
Cocoa powder, to dust

Equipment:

1 mixing bowl   1 palette knife
1 wooden spoon
2 (8-inch) springform pans,
   greased and lined
1 wire rack
1 serving plate

Preparation time: 25 minutes

Cooking time: 20-25 minutes

Serves: 8-10

1. Preheat oven to 350°F (180°C). Then mix together the butter and sugar until creamy.

2. Mix the eggs, yogurt and vanilla extract into the butter mixture. Stir in the flour, baking powder and salt until you have a smooth mixture.

Tilli Tip
★ ★ ★

This cake is best eaten on the day it is made, otherwise the bananas start to turn brown.

3. Divide the mixture between your two pans. Bake for 20-25 minutes, until golden brown.

Store in the fridge when you're not gobbling it up!

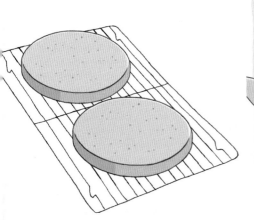

4. Leave the cakes to cool in their pans for 5 minutes. Turn the cakes out onto a wire rack. Peel the paper off then leave to cool completely.

5. Using your palette knife, spread the dulce de leche onto one of the cakes. Top with the sliced banana, reserving some slices for the top layer.

6. Place the other cake on top. Spread with the cream, add more banana slices and dust with cocoa powder.

Fruit Basket Cake

Rating ★★★★

Ingredients:

1 cup (2 sticks) plus 4 tbsp unsalted butter
1 ½ cups granulated sugar
4 large eggs
2 tbsp Greek yogurt
2 cups all-purpose flour
2 tsp baking powder
½ tsp salt
1 jar strawberry jam
2 boxes of chocolate lady fingers or wafers, to decorate
3 large handfuls of fresh fruit, to decorate

For the frosting:

3 cups confectioners' sugar, sifted
½ cup (1 stick) unsalted butter
⅛ tsp salt
1 tbsp strawberry jam

Equipment:

2 mixing bowls   1 palette knife
1 wooden spoon   1 serving plate
1 tablespoon
2 (8-inch) springform pans, greased and lined
1 wire rack

Preparation time: 25 minutes

Cooking time: 20–25 minutes

Serves: 8–10

Try This!
★★★
You can use white or dark chocolate lady fingers, or a mixture of the two to create an eye-catching look.

1. Preheat oven to 350°F (180°C). Mix the butter and sugar together in a large mixing bowl until creamy.

2. Add the eggs and yogurt to the butter mixture. Mix until smooth. Add the flour, baking powder and salt and mix well. Fold in two tablespoons of jam.

3. Divide the batter between the two pans. Bake for 20-25 minutes, until golden brown.

4. Leave the cakes to cool in their pans for 5 minutes. Turn them out onto a wire rack. Peel off the paper and leave to cool completely.

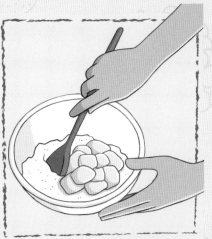

5. Spread one of the cakes with a layer of jam. Place the other cake on top.

6. To make the frosting, put the confectioners' sugar into a mixing bowl. Mix in the butter and salt. Fold in the jam. Using a palette knife, spread the frosting over the top and sides of the cake.

7. Stick the chocolate fingers or wafers around the edge of the cake. Pile the fresh fruit on top.

An impressive cake for a special occasion!

Saucy Chocolate Orange Cake

Rating ★ ★ ★

Ingredients:

1 cup (2 sticks) plus 4 tbsp
   unsalted butter
1 ½ cups granulated sugar
4 free-range eggs
1 ½ cups all-purpose flour
2 ¼ tsp baking powder
1 tsp salt
¼ cup unsweetened
   cocoa powder
Zest of 1 orange
Juice of ½ orange
1 jar orange marmalade
Slice of orange, to decorate

For the frosting:

½ cup semisweet
   chocolate chips
²/₃ cup heavy cream

Equipment:

2 mixing bowls   1 tablespoon
   (1 heatproof)   1 saucepan
1 wooden spoon   1 serving plate
1 whisk
1 zester
1 juicer
2 (8-inch) springform pans,
   greased and lined
1 wire rack

Preparation time: 25 minutes

Cooking time: 20–25 minutes

Serves: 10-12

1. Preheat oven to 350°F (180°C). In a large bowl, mix the butter and sugar together until creamy.

2. Add your eggs to the butter mixture and whisk until light and foamy. Mix in the flour, baking powder, salt and cocoa powder.

3. Mix in the orange zest and juice. Divide the batter between the two lined pans. Bake for 20-25 minutes, until firm to touch.

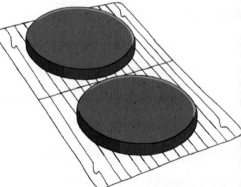

4. Leave the cakes to cool in their pan for 5 minutes. Turn the cakes out onto a wire rack and leave to cool completely. Peel off the paper.

Best eaten while still warm!

Tilli Tip
⭐ ⭐ ⭐

Try stirring your marmalade in a small bowl first to loosen it. This will make it easier to spread onto your cake.

5. Using a tablespoon, spread a layer of marmalade onto one of the cakes. Place the other cake on top.

6. Carefully rest the heatproof bowl over a pan of simmering water. Add the chocolate chips and cream to the bowl. Stir continuously until melted and smooth.

7. Using oven mitts to hold the bowl, pour the chocolate sauce over the cake. Top with an orange slice to finish.

Strawberry Ice Cream Cake

Rating ★ ★ ★

Ingredients:
¼ cup (½ stick) unsalted butter
¼ cup granulated sugar
2 large eggs
2 drops of vanilla extract
¾ cup all-purpose flour
¾ tsp baking powder
¼ tsp salt
Fresh strawberries, to decorate

For the ice cream:
32 small meringue cookies
1 cup sour cream whisked with
   1 cup heavy cream
4 tbsp strawberry jam

Equipment:
2 mixing bowls
1 wooden spoon
1 whisk
1 (9-inch) springform pan,
   greased and lined

Preparation time: 4+ hours

Cooking time: 20–25 minutes

Serves: 8–10

1. Preheat oven to 350°F (180°C). Mix the butter and sugar together in a large mixing bowl until creamy.

2. Whisk the eggs and vanilla extract into the butter mixture. Mix in the flour, baking powder and salt until smooth.

3. Pour the cake batter into the lined pan and bake for 20-25 minutes, until golden brown. Leave the cake in the pan until completely cool.

4. In a small mixing bowl, crush the meringue cookies into small pieces. Gently fold in the cream mixture and jam.

5. Pour the cream mixture on top of the cake in the pan. Tap it against your work surface to make sure it is level. Freeze the cake for at least 4 hours or overnight if possible.

6. Take it out of the freezer 10 minutes before you want to serve it. Release the cake from the pan. Top with fresh strawberries.

Store in the freezer and allow slices to defrost slightly before eating.

Peanut Butter Meringue Cake

Rating ★ ★ ★ ★ ★

Ingredients:
14 tbsp unsalted butter
1 cup granulated sugar
1 ⅓ cups all-purpose flour
½ tsp vanilla extract
3 tbsp Greek yogurt
4 large egg yolks (keep the whites)
2 tsp baking powder

For the meringue:
4 large egg whites
1 ¼ cups granulated sugar

For the filling:
1 ⅔ cups heavy cream, whipped
3 peanut butter and chocolate candybars, chopped
2 cups fresh raspberries

Equipment:
3 large mixing bowls
1 wooden spoon
2 (8-inch) springform pans, greased and lined
1 electric whisk
1 serving plate
1 wire rack
1 spoon

Preparation time: 25 minutes

Cooking time: 30 minutes

Serves: 8–10

1. Preheat oven to 350°F (180°C). Mix the butter and sugar together until creamy. Mix in the yogurt and vanilla extract.

2. Separate four eggs. Set aside the whites, and add the yolks to the butter mixture. Mix well.

3. Add the flour and baking powder. Mix until really smooth. Divide the mixture between the two pans.

4. In a separate bowl, whisk the egg whites with an electric whisk until they are stiff. Gradually whisk in the sugar. Divide the meringue mixture between your two cake pans, carefully smoothing it over the cake batter, to the edges.

Great for a summer party!

Tilli Tip
★ ★ ★
Make sure your bowl is clean and dry when whisking your egg whites, or they won't turn thick and glossy.

5. Bake for 30 minutes, until the meringues are just turning brown. Leave the cakes to cool in the pans for 5 minutes. Carefully transfer the cakes to a wire rack and peel off the paper. Allow the cakes to cool completely.

6. In a mixing bowl, gently whisk the cream until it has thickened. Stir in two of the chopped candybars. Add half the raspberries.

7. Using a spoon, spread most of the cream on one of the cakes. Place the other cake on top. Spoon the rest of the cream on top. Top with the rest of the raspberries and candybar pieces.

Apple Crumble Cake

Rating ★ ★ ★

Ingredients:
½ cup (1 stick) unsalted butter
½ cup packed dark brown sugar
3 large eggs
1 tbsp Greek yogurt
Zest of 1 lemon
1 cup all-purpose flour
1 tbsp baking powder
2 apples, cored and chopped

For the crumble:
½ cup (1 stick) cold
    unsalted butter
⅔ cup all-purpose flour
½ cup granulated sugar
½ cup rolled oats, uncooked
Handful of sunflower seeds

Equipment:
2 large mixing bowls
1 wooden spoon
1 zester
1 (9-inch) springform pan,
    greased and lined
1 spoon
1 serving plate

Preparation time: 25 minutes

Cooking time: 45 minutes

Serves: 8–10

Tilli Tip
★ ★ ★
When making your crumble mixture, don't rub for too long or it will become too sticky and won't crumble well.

1. Preheat oven to 350°F (180°C). Mix the butter and sugar together until creamy.

2. Add the eggs, yogurt and lemon zest to the butter mixture. Mix well. Add the flour and baking powder and mix again until smooth.

3. Pour the batter into a lined cake pan. Sprinkle the chopped apple on the top.

4. To make the crumble, rub together the butter, flour and sugar with your fingers until it looks like breadcrumbs. Gently stir in the oats and seeds.

Delicious served
with vanilla ice cream!

5. Spoon the crumble mixture
over your cake batter. Bake for
35-45 minutes, until golden brown,
and serve while still hot.

Berry and Vanilla Cheesecake

Rating

Ingredients:

1 ¼ cups ginger snaps
6 tbsp unsalted butter, melted
1 cup confectioners' sugar
½ cup sour cream whisked
   with ½ cup heavy cream
1 (16 oz.) container ricotta or
   cottage cheese, drained
1 tsp vanilla extract
2 cups raspberries, strawberries
   or blueberries

Equipment:

1 sandwich or freezer bag
1 rolling pin
2 mixing bowls
1 wooden spoon
1 (9-inch) springform pan,
   greased and lined
1 spoon

Preparation time: 3+ hours

Cooking time: none

Serves: 8–10

1. Place the cookies in a plastic sandwich or freezer bag. Carefully smash the cookies with a rolling pin until they look like crumbs.

2. Tip the cookie crumbs into a small mixing bowl. Add the melted butter and mix well.

3. Tip the cookie mixture into your cake pan. Using your fingers, press the mixture firmly into the base. Refrigerate for 30 minutes to set.

4. In a large mixing bowl, mix together the sugar, cream mixture, ricotta and vanilla extract.

5. Take half of the berries and squash them slightly in your hand. Mix the berries into the cream cheese mixture.

6. Spoon the cream cheese mixture on top of the set biscuit base.

7. Arrange the rest of the berries on top. Refrigerate the cheesecake for at least 3 hours, or overnight if possible. When your cheesecake is set, remove it from the pan and tuck in!

Tilli Tip
★ ★ ★

When crushing cookies, seal the plastic bag so that the crumbs don't fall out.

Index